The Place I Live

The Place I Live
Hub City Kids Write About Home

by the Children
of Spartanburg County

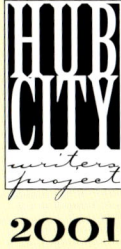

2001

©2001 Hub City Writers Project

All rights reserved. No part of this book may be reproduced in any form or by any electronic or mechanical means including information storage and retrieval systems without permission in writing from the publisher, except by a reviewer, who may quote brief passages in a review.

ISBN 1-891885-20-0
First printing, November 2001

Hub City editors—John Lane & Betsy Wakefield Teter
Art editor—Mark Olencki
Assistant art editor—Helen Correll
Book and cover designs—Mark Olencki
Front cover artwork—Daniel Messick, Chapman Elementary, 2nd grade
Back cover artworks—*Top:* Justyn Jackson, age 9, Jesse S. Bobo Elementary
Bottom: Tyler Brown, age 7, Woodland Heights Elementary
Left: James Sisomseune, age 8, E.P. Todd Elementary
Right: Kacie Hines, age 9, Boiling Springs Elementary
Title page artwork—Amber O'Shields, age 10, Jesse S. Bobo Elementary
Proofreaders—Rachel Farmer & Jill McBurney
Scanning and photography—Christina Smith
Family support—Diana, Weston, Dave, Percysox, Sweety and Sammy
Canine companions—Ellie Mae and Toby
Printed by C&C Offset Printing Co., Ltd. in Tai Po, Hong Kong

Hub City Writers Project
Post Office Box 8421
Spartanburg, South Carolina 29305
(864) 577-9349 • fax (864) 577-0188 • www.hubcity.org

for Bea Bruce

Introduction

There's a belief among the western Apache—the anthropologist Keith Basso has articulated it wonderfully in his book *Wisdom Sits in Places*—that there is a deep connection between native place names and the land itself. Since I first encountered Basso's work, I've always loved this Apache notion that somehow language creates where we are, that a place is tied forever to the names given to it.

To those mostly in charge of naming—real estate developers, city and county commissioners, trustees of large local institutions—the Apache sentiment of attachment must seem archaic at best, romantic and reactionary at worst. In today's market-driven world, names float like some sponsor's blimp above the things they claim. Drive through the growing suburbs of any city and read the signs: names seem cute. Names seem almost random, with no roots dipping into the soil. Among local restaurants, generic is taking over since investors hope to break free of the local and franchise. When planning subdivisions, roads are often named after styles of cars, or Ivy League colleges, or the female relatives of the developer.

Sometimes, though, if we look closely, a local name still summons the spirit of this place we call Spartanburg: I recently cut through the neighborhood bordering Converse College and realized how Blue Ridge Street got its name. From the ridge supporting the street it is possible to see the Blue Ridge looming large thirty miles northwest of the city. "Blue Ridge Street," I whispered, a little bit of wisdom still sitting in place.

This newest Hub City anthology collects the voices of close to 100 young Spartanburg poets and prose writers. Many of the poems are accompanied with artwork as well. The book catches in color the places they live and seals—like one of those insects caught in amber—in verse (and sometimes even in rhyme) their notions of home, of place: Beaumont Park, Pauline, Glendale, Boiling Springs, Silver Lake, Pacolet, Woodruff,

Walnut Grove, Cannons Campground, Cowpens, Enoree (with its whisper of the original Cherokee), Tobe Hartwell, and, my favorite, Lone Oak.

Follow along as our young poets tell us, as Jana Littlejohn does, that "Pauline…smells like grassy fields," and Tiffany Foster at the drag strip remembers "grassy smells/Burning rubber/Fans cheering," and Bryneisha Jeter exclaims in another poem, "There are three trees in my yard!"

I think you'll find it a revelation to read through these pieces of creative writing in *The Place I Live*. These young poets understand naturally that to name is the realm of the poet. They write with passion and accuracy about Spartanburg County, creating a map of places, a chorus of spots and space. The children of Spartanburg still know where wisdom sits.

John Lane
June 2001

Our Hub City

Train whistles blow
Buses rumble
This is our Hub City.

Shoes are clicking
People are talking
This is our Hub City.

Planes depart
And so do we
In our Hub City.

Alexandra Grodzicki
5th Grade • Jesse Boyd Elementary

Amber Andrews
Age 8 • Jesse S. Bobo Elementary

Anna Foster
Age 8 • Jesse S. Bobo Elementary

Kathy Ballenger
3rd Grade • Anderson Mill Elementary

Beaumont Park

The place I love the most is Beaumont Park. I love to see the dust fly all over the guy who tries to field the ball. You better bring a pair of earplugs because the roar of the crowd is as loud as if you were talking through five powerful microphones. My dad buys me a foot long hot dog and he gets a "dodger dog." He devours it in a second. I need a lot of help eating mine. The guys behind us get mad at the players so they throw some peanuts at them. My dad and I reach up and grab some. They don't taste so good.

The ump has to go and change his shirt because someone steals home and gets at least a pound of sand inside his shirt. He wishes he could call him out but the player is safe. You can see it from a mile away. When someone slides everyone gasps, hoping he's either safe or out.

Water drips in the soft sand as the baseball players drink from the marble water fountain. The water drops look like a Dalmatian's spots.

When someone hits a home run the crowd gets up out of their seats and acts like they have never seen a home run before. The teammates jump up in the air like Michael Jordan.

I can't wait to go back to Beaumont Park.

Brandon Griffin
4th Grade
Houston Elementary

Christian Earnhardt
1st Grade
St. Paul's Catholic School

Wild Life at Northside

Motorcycles going down the street like rambling panthers.
People playing music like elephants having a stampede.
Babies crying like an old granny taking out her false teeth.
People slamming their screen doors like people blowing their horns.
People talking like dogs barking.
Children playing and screaming like they're at the fair on a scary ride.
Police creeping by like no one heard them, very quiet!

Terrica Mullins
6th Grade • Cleveland Elementary

Jasmine Lyles
Age 6 • Wellford Elementary

Mike Dyson
Age 10
Woodruff Elementary

Pauline

Pauline is the color green.
It tastes like fried chicken.
It sounds like dogs barking and cows mooing.
It smells like grassy fields.
It looks like horses grazing and cows snoozing.
Pauline makes me feel like I could just sleep the day away.

Jana Littlejohn
3rd Grade • Pauline-Glenn Springs Elementary

Glendale

My neighborhood isn't too big, but it isn't too small either. My neighborhood is not rich at all. At the end of the street that I live on there's a big white mansion that is abandoned. Some people think that it's haunted, but I don't. Glendale is an historical place. They have even saved buildings that are about one hundred years old. The church that I go to is more than one hundred years old, but I'm not surprised it hasn't fallen in yet. There isn't really anything new in Glendale. That's what my neighborhood is like.

Jonathan Bryant
5th Grade • Clifdale Elementary

Old Tub

I remember my brother and cousins.
I remember an old tub in the woods.
I remember playing around in the old tub in the woods.
I remember my oldest cousin and his friends flipped the tub.
I remember being furious.

I remember growing up.
I remember leaving the tub.
I remember visiting again but being chased off by a pack of dogs.

Jacob Collins
5th Grade • O. P. Earle Elementary

Kevin Gossett
Age 12 • Cannons Elementary

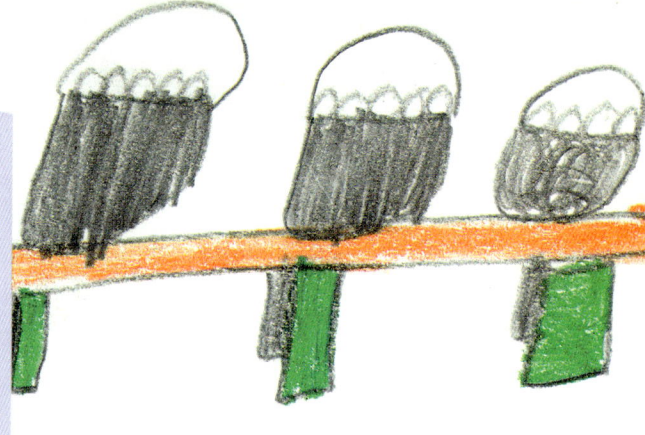

I Am A Peach Tree

I am a peach tree.
I am very stiff before the wind blows my leaves.
I feel a tingle on my branch.
It is a tiger swallowtail butterfly.
My fruit is very plump and juicy.
I am ready to be picked.
I am glad I am a peach tree.

Latisha Lynch
3rd Grade • Chapman Elementary

Andrew Estes
Age 9 • Houston Elementary

John Gasque
Age 10 • Woodruff Elementary

My Farm

My farm is special because we have so many cows. We have about three hundred fifty of them. They are milked at one o'clock in the morning and one o'clock in the afternoon. There is a bunch of them, so we have a really big barn. We have a milk room where we milk them. Sometimes it stinks at my farm.

We have baby calves, mama cows, and bulls. We also have many tractors. Sometimes we have to feed the baby calves in the morning and in the afternoon.

We have other animals too. We have many dogs, three horses, and a pony. We have huge fields where the animals can run around.

We enjoy living and working on a farm.

Whitney Palmer
2nd Grade • Pauline-Glenn Springs Elementary

Silver Lake

Markeisha Nesbitt
Age 8 • Houston Elementary

The place I live is near Silver Lake. It is a very large lake. I live in a trailer near the lake. Silver Lake got its name from the silvery light that always shines. John A. Silver was a great explorer who built a grand old stable. The stable is now abandoned. I live near Berry Shoals Road. My trailer is very gray. My home has trees, grass, and even the lake.

Holden Brewington
4th Grade
Reidville Elementary

Boiling Springs

Hello I'm Billy
The Boiling Springs.
I'm nothing but
An old bubbly thing.
I can't play games,
I'm not athletic,
I can't do anything.
I'm so pathetic.
You see
My life is the worst of them all.
I used to live happily,
And I had a ball.
The woods was the place
I wanted to stay.
They were very peaceful,
Day after day.
The woods were beautiful
The greenery and scrubs,
I remember the kids
That used us for tubs.
The days would go by
Just so very quick,
And the only things in me
Were a leaf or a stick.
The woods were the best thing,
That ever happened to me.
If you lived there
You'd probably see.
But now it's so different,
It's changed so much
It's like a magical fairy
Created an evil touch.
One day these people,
They chopped down the trees,
I was so scared.
What would they do with me?
It turned out they did nothing with me.
They just left me here
For people to see.

Everyone thinks the beginning is worst
But actually
It wasn't so bad at first.
I'm so miserable
The days go by slow, do I live a good life?
My answer is no.
I have trash in me now,
Trash galore,
All kinds of trash
That comes from the store.
I'll never be happy
Unless they do what they should.
Give me my old life
And put back the woods.
On cold days I'm cold,
On hot days I'm hot,
Will I always be miserable?
I hope not!
I'm done with complaining.
It doesn't help a thing,
To occupy time
I'm just gonna sing.
"God please help me
I hate to complain
But if things stay like this
I might go insane.
I hope that my life will change
That would be great,
But I guess I'll be patient
And I'll just have to wait."

Nicholas Millwood
5th Grade • Boiling Springs Elementary

Hayden Clarke
Age 11 • Holly Springs-Motlow Elementary

The thing I like about spartanburg is my teacher Mrs. Byce!

Jamaar Meadows
Age 11 • Pauline-Glenn Springs Elementary

Mary Ashleigh Browning
Age 7 • Woodland Heights Elementary

I Am

I am a citizen of Spartanburg.
I wonder what will happen to our grand city.
I hear it is the land of the free.
I want no one to be a slave.
I am a citizen of Spartanburg.

I pretend that no one litters in our lovely city.
I feel sorry for animals that get abused.
I touch the red soil of the Piedmont.
I worry about what the future holds for us.
I cry out, "Be proud of this city!"
I am a citizen of Spartanburg.

I understand we should have rights.
I say, "We should not fight."
I dream that we will have peace among people.
I try to be a good citizen of our city.
I hope that things will change for the better.
I am a citizen of Spartanburg.

Petho Theuambounmy
4th Grade • E. P. Todd Elementary

Nathalie Emplit
5th Grade • Anderson Mill Elementary

Tesse Arreola
Age 8 • Fairforest Elementary

Pacolet River

The water is a ball rolling on the rocks,
The deer are suspicious detectives looking for a crime.
The fish are pieces of tinfoil shooting through the water.
The smell of roses and skunks.
The River.

Landon Champion
5th Grade • Cannons Elementary

Autum Jones
Age 10 • Cowpens Elementary

Jeanette Bates
Age 9 • Woodland Heights Elementary

The Clock Tower

Oh, the clock tower
Standing up so high
Blending with clouds and
Sky
Wonder why they
Worked so hard,
To give you such
Height
When if made shorter
Could easily be wound
Tight.

Adrian Smart
5th Grade • Houston Elementary

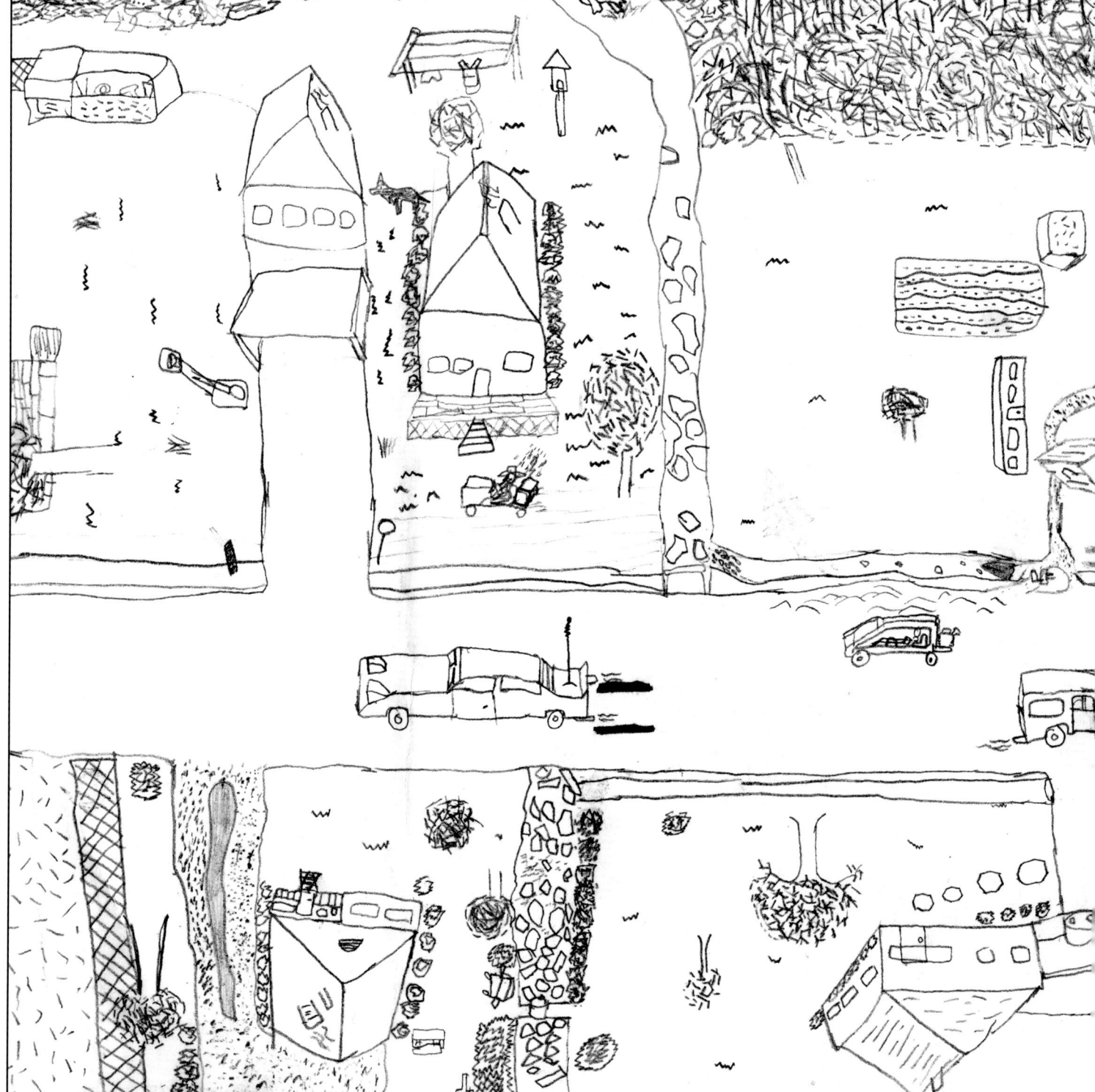

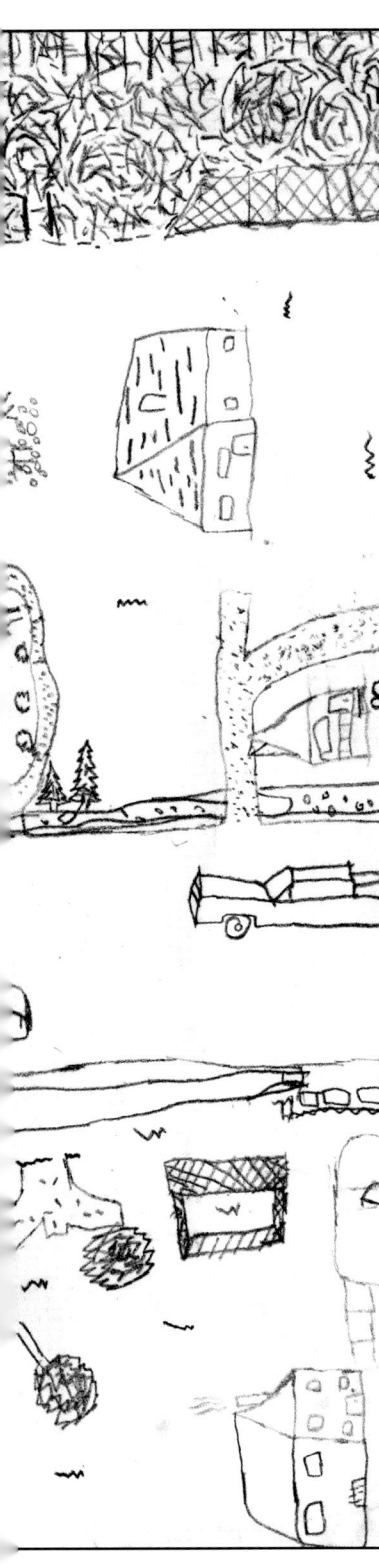

Chris Arthur
Age 11 • Houston Elementary

I Hear

Birds chirping while sitting in a tree
Clocks ticking when the bells are ringing
Floors rattling when trucks pass by
Trash cans clanging when being put down.

Kids hiding while playing hide-n-seek
Moms yelling to get kids in the house
Doors slamming when kids come
Phones ringing and people chattering.

Guns shooting, people getting killed
People crying 'cause they've heard of the young one dying
Feet moving to a rhythm
Drums beating to the beat of the heart.

Cats meowing, dogs barking
Cars passing, kids walking
People coming and some going
Not always returning.

I hear.

Kiarra Boyd
6th Grade • Park Hills Elementary

Dear Friend,

    Hi, my name is DeOnté Norman. I am writing you to tell you about my city in the year 2000. My city's name is Spartanburg in South Carolina. In South Carolina we have good schools, like my school, Anderson Mill Elementary. We have lovely teachers like my teacher Miss Johnson. She is nice and very pretty.
    In South Carolina we have good people and bad people. I'm a good person. My family are good people too. I don't like bad people. Some of them are so bad they have to go jail. Jail is a place where bad people go to when they are bad. Make sure that you are not bad.
    My favorite place in South Carolina is the mall. That's a place where you go to buy your stuff like shoes, shirts, and pants. My favorite food place is at my house. I love my mom's cooking. In the year 2100 I hope you have a good life like me. Bye!!!

Your friend,

DeOnté Norman
4th Grade • Anderson Mill Elementary

Doughnuts

I went to Krispy Kreme.

I heard orders being taken and the chattering of little girls.

I smelled the sweet smell of sticky frosting being poured over the freshly baked doughnuts.

I saw the round, crisp, chocolaty doughnuts.

I felt the smooth, sweet doughnut melt in my mouth and the coolness of my drink.

Rebecca McCarter
6th Grade • Chapman Elementary

Paolo Arce
5th Grade • Anderson Mill Elementary

The Place I Live

C   is for churches.
O   is for some of the old buildings.
W   is for some of the warehouses.
P   is for our post office.
E   is for the places we go to eat.
N   is for the new library we'll have.
S   is for the beautiful stars we can see at night.

Kayla Edge
4th Grade • Cowpens Elementary

Belvedere

I live in a neighborhood called Belvedere. Lots of my friends live there. My house is made out of bricks. I have a playhouse in my backyard. It is quiet in my neighborhood. My house is close to my school. I live with my mom and my dad and my sister and my baby brother. One day I want to live in a big hotel that has a swimming pool.

Melonie Trinh
1st Grade • Arcadia Elementary

Anna Grace Long
Age 9 • Fairforest Elementary

Alex Hauldrook
Age 7 • Westview Elementary

Nicholas Bullman
Age 9 • Jesse S. Bobo Elementary

Kaitlyn Bush
Age 7 • Woodland Heights Elementary

*Ian Compton
Age 10
Cowpens
Elementary*

Crossroads

I go to the crossroads at my grandma's house
The lake is like a dirty bathtub full of water
The cows are like hairy statues
The grass is like tons of grasshoppers in a row standing on their hind legs
The clouds look like stretched marshmallows before I put them on a stick to roast them
when I make s'mores
The flowers smell like my sister's green apple shampoo
The crossroads at my grandma's house make me feel as happy as when you hit a grand slam
to win the championship

*Hunter Brown
6th Grade • Spartanburg Day School*

The Great Magnolia Tree of Woodruff

A long, long time ago there was a tree that stood 65 feet high. This was one historic tree. This tree was a Magnolia. A man named Capt. Andrew Woodruff brought back a seedling from Sullivan's Island. This was the time of the War, the War Between the States.

The Daughters of the American Revolution wrote a book about it called *Trees of Fame*. The tree was 12 feet in circumference, and was known as the "The Tree of the Universe." This tree was planted in 1862 and cut down in the name of Progress to build antique stores in Woodruff.

Brittany Varner
5th Grade • Woodruff Elementary

Quentin Zorn
5th Grade • O.P. Earle Elementary

Brittany Green
Age 10 • Wellford Elementary

Recipe for City Industrial Zone

Ingredients:
Factories | Power plants
Train cars | Trucks
Train tracks | Warehouses

Place three factories on the ground.
Spread on train tracks.
Sprinkle 20 train cars on the tracks.
Set 10 power plants on the cement.
Pour the 200 trucks on the road.
Roll 7 more warehouses on the ground.
Mix all together.
Bake at 350 degrees and then you will have an industrial zone.

Cassie Losey
3rd Grade • Wellford Elementary

Recipe for City Residential Zone

Ingredients:
Houses | Grocery Store
Park | Bank
School | Land
Restaurants

Set up some land.
Season the land with houses.
Sprinkle in a park.
Place in a school.
Knead in a grocery store.
Decorate it with a restaurant.
Glaze it with a bank.
Bake at 350 degrees and you will get a residential city zone.

Brittany Hart
3rd Grade • Wellford Elementary

Brianna McKinney
Age 7 • Cannons Elementary

A Place I Would Like to Live

I would like to live in a place where I could go outside and play and not be scared. I would like to have kids my age to play with, so they could come to my house. I could go to their house, and we could ride our bikes. I want to live somewhere where people don't walk down the street drinking beer, and where they don't sell drugs. I want to live somewhere safe.

Dylan Horton
2nd Grade • Arcadia Elementary

My House

My house is great
My house is fine
My house is super
My house is divine

9 windows last count
with a kitchen so sweet
my mom and dad's room
which is so clean and neat

I think my room's the best
My sister's room is too
She has bright pink walls
And mine are navy blue

3 bedrooms and 2 bathrooms
and only 1 den
and food and dessert
inside the kitchen

that is my place
my house my home
with friends and family
the best place to roam

Matthew Helderman
5th Grade
Fairforest Elementary

Stephanie Faircloth
Age 10
Pauline-Glenn Springs Elementary

My Three Trees

There are three trees in my yard! I like my three trees. When my friends come over we play in the trees. I like trees to play with. My two sisters and my brother live with me. We can swing from the trees. My house and the trees are both brown now. Soon the trees will be green. It will be spring and the wind will blow the trees.

Bryneisha Jeter
Kindergarten • Z. L. Madden Elementary

Cannons Campground

I live in Cannons Campground. I live in a gray house. The road I live on is Old Converse Road. I live right across the street from my school. My school is blue. I have to go to my daddy's. And my other house is light brown. And my other house is in Gaffney.

Quinton Smiley
1st Grade • Cannons Elementary

The Place I Live

My town has a place called Bronco's. They speak Spanish there and I do, too. I eat tacos when I go there.

Angie Garza
Kindergarten • Cowpens Elementary

My Tree

Since I have lived in cities all my life, I never had a tree to play on until we moved to Spartanburg. I don't usually see a tree this big. It has fallen down across a creek. My friends and I call it "Old Chunky." You can jump on it if you're not scared, or just sit, talk, or think. When I look down from the tree, I see something beautiful. It's life—a green creek, plants, and minnows. It's life just how I like it!

Jack Kurczy
3rd Grade • Pine Street Elementary

Rebekah Morgan
Age 8 • Roebuck Elementary

Chelsea Bagwell
Age 10
Roebuck Elementary

Trottin' Sally

In the 1920's there was a man named Trottin' Sally who loved to play the violin. He got his name because he loved to go up and down the town of Spartanburg playing his violin. Every day people listened to his music on the street corners. Sometimes they gave him a penny or two. He was a nice man and he could play the violin very well. Sometimes the children would even listen to his music. Spartanburg was lucky to have a man like him.

Dwayne Garrett
3rd Grade • Chapman Elementary

Dear Friend,

    I'm writing to tell you (whoever you are) what Spartanburg is like in 2000. It is cool. Is it in 2100? You must have incredible technology. Do you have hovercrafts? Do you have monorail systems? Those are just ideas of what good technology you all have.

    Five good things in my life in 2000 are video games, school, church, people, and Mountasia. Video games are amusing. School, well, we have the best schools in the country. Church is enjoyable. The people are very nice. And Mountasia is a fun park.

    Five bad things we have are pollution, smoking, drunk driving, criminals, and people without homes. Pollution is really bad for the air. Smoking can kill people. Drunk driving makes you drive bad and crash. Criminals are usually caught, though. The homeless must be miserable.

    My favorite things are home, Putt-Putt, golf, bowling, and sports. Home rocks the house because you're with your family. Putt-putt is fun, and I play lots of sports, including bowling. Bye!

Sincerely,

Kevin Lybrand
4th Grade • Anderson Mill Elementary

Laney Talbert
Age 11 • Pine Street Elementary

Life At Walnut Grove

My name is Thomas Moore. I live at Walnut Grove. I help my dad work on the farm and I help him in the garden. We are planting tomatoes, corn, beans, potatoes, and cabbage. I sleep on a feather bed upstairs. My mom does all of the housework. My dad and I work from 5:00 in the morning until 12:00 noon. Then we take a break and eat lunch. Then we start back and work until late afternoon. It is a lot of work but I don't mind. I love working at Walnut Grove with my dad.

Zoey Classen
3rd Grade • Chapman Elementary

Jennifer Gaida
Age 9 • Roebuck Elementary

Heartland - My Home

My home the Heartland is great and white.
Lots of farms all tied up tight.
Hear the rooster wake up the day.
I live that life, that's just my way.

Watch the children laugh and play.
The city is small, but buildings tall.
Lots of people raise hogs and cows.
Hear the big machines roar and plow.

A life like this is sometimes hard.
But when you look out the windows you see so far.
People pray every day that no blizzard will come.
That's the life of my home—the Heartland.

Zachary Lawson
3rd Grade • Duncan Elementary

Boiling Springs

Rabbit, fox, deer
Soccer, football, track, basketball
Marlowe & Company, Ingles, Wal-Mart, Eckerd's
Zaxby's, Panda Chinese, La Fogata, Coby's, McDonald's
Boiling Springs First Baptist, Boiling Springs Church of Christ
Helpful, caring, generous, kind, loving, friendly people
Peaches, corn, beans, okra, tomatoes
Hwy 9, Rainbow Lake Road, I-85
Rivers, lakes, streams
My Home Town

Brittney Lindsey
4th Grade • Boiling Springs Elementary

Donna McGee
Age 11 • Woodruff Elementary

Casey Wellingsky
Age 6
River Ridge Elementary

A. J. Hughes
Age 10
West View Elementary

Planters Walk

I live in the Planters Walk subdivison.
There has never been a car collision.

I live in the middle of a cul-de-sac.
It is packed full of children.

We enjoy playing with our friends.
We wish the days would never end.

I enjoy our neighborhood pool.
In the summer, it keeps us cool.

In the fall, I rake up the leaves.
In the winter, we have a big freeze.

In the spring, we enjoy the dandelions blowing in the breeze.
I bet you could have guessed, of all the seasons, I like summer the best.

Ryan MacMillan
3rd Grade • Fairforest Elementary

Country Life

Why I love the Country Life
It's simple as can be
Here are just a few things
That Country means to me.

I love how the Country sounds
All night and all day
Like the birds singing in the morning
And at night the frogs at play.

I love to hear a Whippoorwill
And the wind blow through the trees
Or the chirping of the crickets
And the buzz of Bumble Bees.

I also love the crunching
Of the leaves beneath my feet
Or the rumble of the tractor
As I climb upon the seat.

I love to hear the flowing
Of the water in a creek
Or the sound of children giggling
As they're playing hide-n-seek.

But the one thing that I love the most
That makes Country Life so grand
Is a long walk down a Country Road
With my Daddy hand in hand.

Amanda Harris
5th Grade • Boiling Springs Elementary

Battle of Cowpens

It was early in the morning at 8:00 on January 17, 1781. Daniel Morgan was the leader of the colonists. Morgan knew his men were afraid of Banastre Tarleton so he lined his men in three rows. First was the Sharpshooters, next was the Militia men, and last the Continental soldiers. Morgan told his men to fire two shots. He said to move back in the next row right after the two shots. The Continental soldiers misunderstood the order and started to run. Morgan won the battle!

Dylan Rudicill
3rd Grade • Cowpens Elementary

Darryn Gilbert
6th Grade
Z. L. Madden Elementary

Indian Burial Grounds

Ghosts of Indians streak around
My house and forest,
Turning and squeaking our chimney cover.
They also cause our lank, old trees
To creak as they rush past,
Even when the wind is calm.

Once, as I was strolling through my woods,
My foot fell through a large mound.
I was so frightened I ran away
As fast as I could.
Sometimes late at night
I hear the restless ghosts
Of Indians creeping around
Inside my house.

Now, I am very cautious around my new home,
For there are Indian Burial Grounds in my own woods.

Regina Dillinger
5th Grade • O. P. Earle Elementary

Hearse

Glossy, black, and spooky
Death Kingdom automobile
Lies in the forest's depths near my house.

Boys hitting golf balls—
Broken windows.
Only source of outside life gone
Crushing thousands of memories.
Spirits resting in peace awaken.
Glass replaced.
Soon to be removed to its final resting place—
A scrap yard.

Grim Reaper in the form of a tow truck
Comes to take it for its last ride.

T. J. Vaughn
5th Grade • O. P. Earle Elementary

The Place I Live

The place I live is between Cowpens and Pacolet. I live in a very peaceful area. There are two houses beside my house. One is on one side and the other is on the other side. So you would say I live in the middle. I have a very big yard, and very few trees. I love my yard because I have a lot of room.

There is a fire department near my house. The name of the fire department is Glendale. It is the newest Glendale Fire Department. I enjoy looking at the fire trucks ride by my house.

My favorite place to eat that's near my house is Mullinax's. I love eating hot dogs, chicken tenders, and cheeseburgers. My family owns Mullinax's. I go there a lot with my family to eat. They make the best pies. It's wonderful to have Mullinax's so close to me. I love their food.

My school is about 5 minutes away from my house. The name of my school is Clifdale Elementary. All my friends are in my class. My teacher's name is Mrs. Bridges. She is really nice. I love my school.

The place I live is very peaceful. I enjoy living where I live. I hope I will never have to move!

Alysia Brown
4th Grade • Clifdale Elementary

Ishayda Hughes
Age 6 • River Ridge Elemementary

A Walk on Raintree Drive

Dogs speeding across the road
Like cheetahs to catch a cat.
Police sirens as loud as
a lion's roar.
Kids riding bikes
and scooters extremely wild.
People fighting with great animosity.
Ice-cream man slowly driving by.
Teenagers laughing like hyenas.
Kids enjoying themselves greatly.

Kwame Myers
6th Grade • Cleveland Elementary

Jordan Dowdle
Age 5 • Duncan Elementary

Todd Watkins
Age 11
Woodland Heights
Elementary

Spartanburg

Sunny
Polite
Awesome
Roebuck is in it
Traffic sometimes
Airports
Nice looking
Bizarre things
Usually quiet
Rains sometimes
Great place to live

Jason Morriss
5th Grade • Roebuck Elementary

Brittany Brown
6th Grade
Houston Elementary

Life on Southern Avenue

Children playing like baboons in a tree.
Birds singing like rap stars on the street.
People cutting grass like trucks on a track.
Children swimming like they are on a swim team.
People playing ball like NBA stars.

Syerra Simpson
6th Grade • Cleveland Elementary

The Best Day

I went to the Pacolet River on Sunday.
I felt a speck of rain on my face.
It felt like an ice cube.
At the dam, I heard water banging
like a drum on the rocks.
I smelled fish.
I heard cars going by me.
I saw the sun trying to get out,
but the rain kept hitting my face.
I knew the gate was going to open again.
Then I left the river.

Cameron Jones
4th Grade • Clifdale Elementary

Christina Davis
Age 8
Duncan Elementary

The Beacon

I remember the loud shouts,
almost like fire engines,
and the smells of grease and steam.

I remember crunching on fries
that seemed like firecrackers
exploding in the air.

I remember wanting a hamburger
that came as big as a balloon.
Then I would go outside
and see the flags waving in the air
like the sails of a ship.

Brooks Cochran
5th Grade • Pine Street Elementary

Aaron Case
6th Grade • Chapman Elementary

My House

I can see
Lots of flowers,
but no towers.
A huge lake,
and a yellow rake.
Lots of plants,
and some ants.
A big flagpole,
and a small ant hole.
I see my dog,
and sometimes a frog.
My two cats,
but not any bats.

Marie Hannouche
4th Grade
St. Paul's Catholic School

Carolina Wrens

There are
Carolina Wrens
In my yard
All day long

They eat on my suet feeder all day long.
The song they sing sounds like the tea kettle.
The tail stands right up when they're excited.
I like to sneak up and watch them play.
They fly away at the end of the day.
It's wonderful to watch the
Carolina Wrens.

Zella Classen
3rd Grade • Chapman Elementary

Cortney Nance
Age 7 • Fairforest Elementary

Enoree

I live in a little town called Enoree. It doesn't have any red lights yet. It could be the smallest town in South Carolina. It's not a real hi-tech town. You have to go there to know what I'm talking about. We have words like ye, meaning you or your. We use it in sentences like "Get ye hot dog and leave." Actually, we have names for some of the places in Enoree even if it is small. The James Nesbitt plantation house is the oldest plantation house in the Upstate. There was even a hotel in Enoree. Its name was The Old Enoree Hotel. It was founded in 1875 and it burned down in the late 1930s. That is what the place I live is like.

Jake Hennett
4th Grade • Woodruff Elementary

Sadie Goodwin
Age 9
Boiling Springs Elementary

Joshua Smith
1st Grade • Roebuck Elementary

Tobe Hartwell

I live in Spartanburg. I live in an apartment. I live in Tobe Hartwell. They put something new that will give us shade so if the sun comes out we can stay cool. It is a shield.

We have a football field. My next door neighbor is nice. She gives us candy every time she gets it. First we have to ask her then we get it.

Tobe Hartwell is safe. I like living there.

Kwame Fernanders
1st Grade • Z. L. Madden Elementary

In My House and Neighborhood

In my house there are marvelous toys!
 In my neighborhood there are kids making noise.
In my house we are having fun.
 In my neighborhood everyone is in the sun.
In my house my cousin is eating ice.
 In my neighborhood people are being nice.
In my house my sister is quiet as a mouse.
 In my neighborhood people are running in the house.
In my house my brothers are flying to bed.
 In my neighborhood friends are in a race and getting ahead.
In my house kids are running like a cheetah.
 In my neighborhood kids saying, "I'll bet I'll beat you."
In my house Granny is sleeping like a polar bear.
 In my neighborhood girls are brushing their hair.
In my house Granny is eating corn.
  In my neighborhood my mom is blowing her horn.
In my house there are fun things to do like visiting a jungle or a zoo.
 But wait my neighborhood is fun too.

Nikita Farr
6th Grade • Cleveland Elementary

Alex Hy
4th Grade • Z. L. Madden Elementary

Scotsgrove Stables

My favorite thing to do in South Carolina is horseback ride. I horseback ride at Scotsgrove Stables in Inman, South Carolina. There I have learned how to ride English style, jump over hurdles and jumps and canter on a horse for the first time. My favorite thing to do at Scotsgrove is go on long trail rides. On our trail rides we go over fields and through apple orchards. Sometimes we ride along a creek in the forest and on really hot days we go through the creek to cool off the horses. Sometimes we get a little cooled off too!

Kelly Salyer
6th Grade • Holly Springs-Motlow Elementary

Dear Friend (in the Year 2100),

100 years before you moved to this neighborhood it had a lot of dogs in it. I also had a dog. Whenever I took her on a walk, all the neighborhood dogs started to bark. There were a lot of parts to this neighborhood. I don't know about now. I loved it then, and I probably still would.

Sincerely,

Pallavi Kumar
4th Grade • Anderson Mill Elementary

Sara Workman
Age 8 • River Ridge Elementary ▶

The Cliff

I went to the cliff behind my house in the woods with my friend. He brought a rope. He tied it around the tree. It looked like a snake. The tree bark looked like beef jerky. I started down the cliff. The rope felt like little spikes. The sky looked as blue as blueberries. The tree's sap smelled like waffles. I heard crows call nearby. I saw bees flying by. I climbed back up, then we left.

Isaac White
4th Grade
Clifdale Elementary

Cowpens

In my community there are woods. In the woods up on a hill the army battled there once. There is a hole in the ground and my stepdad said it leads to China. It looks dirty. He said he went in it when he was a teenager.

I have friendly neighbors. I live in a neighborhood. I have a bed and a blanket to keep me warm. A little church is close to me. There is a bridge close to me. There are rivers close to me.

Alexis Bailey
1st Grade
Cowpens Elementary

Ryan Fowler
Age 5 • Houston Elementary

Andy Gray
5th Grade • Anderson Mill Elementary

My House

I live on Ridge Road.
29365 is my zip code.
My house is three stories high.
Sometimes my brother and I have to clean inside.

There are two animals that live in my house.
My dog, my cat, but not a mouse.
I only have one brother.
I'm glad I don't have another.

The basement in my house is pretty cool.
But I still wish we had a pool.
My dad collects things and puts them on the basement walls.
He also collects baseballs and footballs.

I like the main level the least.
When we have company that's where we feast.
There are two TVs on the main floor.
There are also two doors.

I like the upstairs the best.
I also like it when we have guests.
I like climbing out the window and jumping to the grass.
After I jump, I hope I never have to wear a cast.

A. J. Simpson
4th Grade • Duncan Elementary

Under My House

    I like to play under my house when I am mad. The grass is forest green. The trees are misty brown. The sky is light blue. The mud is dark red. The flowers are lemon yellow. Under my house I hear footsteps, meowing, barking, and yelling. Under my house I see worms, ants, bugs, and flowers. It is big up under my house. I love it up under my house. When I am not mad anymore, I come out. I love it there because it helps me get unmad.

Josh Barnes
3rd Grade • Jesse S. Bobo Elementary

Meghan Blick
Age 9
Roebuck Elementary

Where I Live

I live in a white house. My house is surrounded by a fence with a dog in it. I live by a skate park, a baseball park, and a regular park. There is a lot of fresh air where I live. I live by a church, but it is not the church that I go to. My address is 195 Boundary Drive. There is a wicker chair on my porch. In my backyard, there is a basketball hoop, a parking lot, a shed which holds skates, bikes, and other junk, and ramps for biking and skating. There are also a lot flowers.

I live in Spartanburg, S.C. There are a lot of schools, malls, restaurants, shops, lakes, houses, children, people, churches, gyms, bridges, cars, zoos, parks, pet stores, trees, polluted air, bikes, and any thing else you can name. I have lived in Spartanburg for eleven years. I love where I live.

N. Chenalle Dew
5th Grade • Houston Elementary

Travis Bailey
Age 7
Fairforest Elementary

Jason Morriss
Age 11 • Roebuck Elementary

Marylee Martin
Age 7 • Pine Street Elementary

The Drag Strip

Eager racers
Popcorn poppin'
Food cooking
Passing animals
Heating tires
Motors revvin'
Car exhaust
Gassy smells
Burning rubber
Fans cheering
Lights flashing
Tires spinnin'
Rumbling benches
Announcing winners
Sleepy people
Heading home

Tiffany Foster
5th Grade • Fairforest Elementary

Where Did I Go?

I went to my uncle's workshop.
I heard the banging of the tires falling
to the floor.
I smelled the coffee roaming in the air.
I saw a very neat old car.
I felt the vibrations of the engines
under my feet.

Jordan Henderson
3rd Grade • Wellford Elementary

Bellamy Purinton
Age 11 • Pine Street Elementary ▶

Noises in the Morning

When I get up every morning
I go outside and get the paper.
Sometimes my dog chews it up.
I hear dogs in the morning. I hear
construction. I hear rushing water.
You would not believe all that
I hear.

Caitlyn Culp
3rd Grade • Hendrix Elementary

Maggie Lowery
Age 7 • Cannons Elementary

My House

In my house the rules are complicated. My grandmother makes the rules since she is the oldest grownup. She makes me realize it is important to be safe.

My parents and I play Uno and Twister. We have a wonderful time together. We laugh and one time I did a flip because I was very excited. I broke my grandmother's lamp. That is why she made the rules. Even though we have lots of rules to be safe, it is still exciting at my house.

Tristam Browning
2nd Grade • Hendrix Elementary

Ariel Batchelor
Age 8
E. P. Todd Elementary

The Stable

I remember my old stable
The horses sound like children on a jungle gym
Feed smelled as sweet as maple syrup
The cats chasing the mice look like streaks on the floor
The heater sounds like monsters waking up

Katie Burke
6th Grade • Spartanburg Day School

Walnut Grove

I went to Walnut Grove.
I heard birds' wings flapping.
I smelled burned candle wax.
I saw old dirty houses and a sign saying
  "Beware of Ants."
I felt dried candle wax and a beat up fence.

Travis Trojan
2nd Grade • Houston Elementary

Leah Rogers
Age 6 • Reidville Elementary

Mikki Brooks
Age 6
Duncan Elementary

Barnet Park

My favorite place is Barnet Park.

You can run in the spout.
You can scream and shout.

You can make friends there.
You can wear funky hair.

You can have a picnic lunch.
You can drink and munch.

You can listen to favorite music with your ears.
You can play ball on a day sunny and clear.

My favorite place is Barnet Park.

Adam Hopkins
3rd Grade • Jesse S. Bobo Elementary

Emily Bowie
Age 9
Woodland Heights Elementary

Little Pink Anderson

The Blues made me happy.
It was a good time.
I tried to shout.
I was acting silly.
I wiggled 14 times.
I wanted to go on the stage!
Little Pink Anderson gave me a hug.

Tyler Cohen
1st Grade • Houston Elementary

My Antique House

I don't know exactly when my house was built, but I do know it has some history. My Great Great Aunt Susie lived in this house many years ago. My grandmother told me so. My Aunt Shirley gave us the house in August this past year. She decided she needed a bigger house.

The first thing neat I noticed about my house was the keyholes. They were different than those where I used to live, and the key was funny that fit in the holes. I wondered what the house would look like beyond the doors with the funny keyholes. I wondered if the rooms would be strange, but when I stepped into the rooms, they were huge with bright shiny floors. I soon found out my house had five rooms: a bathroom, two bedrooms, a kitchen, and a living room.

I have a nice room all to myself. It's got white walls and a tan carpet. I'm so happy to be home. I don't think about going anywhere else. But if I wanted to go somewhere, my house is on Oakdale Court right behind the post office, so I could walk to downtown Spartanburg. I wouldn't want to live anywhere else.

Chris Smith
5th Grade • Z. L. Madden Elementary

James McVey
Age 5 • River Ridge Elementary

The Greek Festival in Spartanburg

The most important thing about the Greek Festival
Is that you have fun!
It is full of delicious smells.
Sometimes you will see Greek dancers.
People come from all over town to see it.
There are lots of things to buy.
It has games for the children.
There are tours of the church.
It is great every year!
But the most important thing about the Greek Festival
Is to have fun!

Christina Nayfa
5th Grade • Jesse Boyd Elementary

Taylor Strange
Age 6
Roebuck Elementary

Chelsea Thompson
Age 8
West View Elementary

At Hollywild Zoo

At Hollywild Zoo I hear all kinds of racket!
I hear the elephant howling for food.
I listen to the gorilla screeching with anger.
I hear the otter gargling with joy!
I hear the hyena laughing at the cheetah that fell with a loud yelp!
I hear the camel smacking his ripe, green grass.
I hear the goats licking their milk.
I listen to the chimpanzees shake the bars.
I hear my mom calling "Nathan!"
I get into the car with a thud.
We drive off with a screech!!

Nathan Branch
3rd Grade • Wellford Elementary

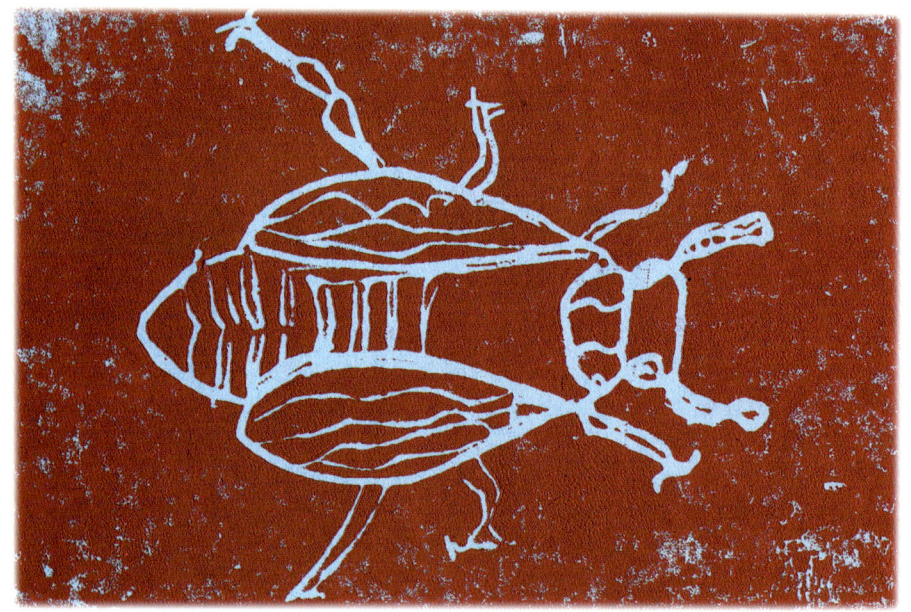

Lake Cooley

My brothers and I go to a lake near Spartanburg. It is called Lake Cooley. The water in the lake is very clear, and we can see the mountains purple in the distance. Lake Cooley has lots of seagulls flying in the air getting their food. Seagulls usually live in the sea, not in a town that is 250 miles away. There was a storm that blew the seagulls from the ocean to our town many years ago. It was called Hurricane Hugo.

The lake is fed by streams nearby. There are crawfish that live in these streams. You can find them by looking carefully at the rocks in the water. If you see a crawfish, you pick up the rock, then quickly catch the crawfish with your two hands. We put our crawfish in a bucket, and take them home with us. Once we caught sixty or seventy. My mom and dad boil a big pot of water, and put the crawfish in until they are cooked. The are delicious to eat with salt, pepper, and butter.

My brothers and I go fishing there with our parents, and catch bluegills, bass, catfish, and bream. Once we caught a very big bass. All of the fish we catch are good to eat. We also like to just run around and look for the places where the fish live. There is a playground there at the lake, and we like to swing on the monkeybars there. We have been coming to this lake for as long as we can remember. It is a great place for us!

Sean Yang, 1st Grade
Steven Yang, 2nd Grade
Cher Fue Yang, 4th Grade
Lone Oak Elementary

Top: *De Foster*
Age 8 • Duncan Elementary

Right: *Andre Gentry*
Age 7 • E. P. Todd Elementary

Lakeview Manor

I live in Lakeview Manor
Shootouts
Fights
And bad attitudes
Life is bad here.

Brittany Fair
3rd Grade • Cannons Elementary

The Spartanburg Little Theatre

At last the curtain rises,
And the first performance begins.
After all of that work and practice,
The hard part finally ends.

You are a little nervous,
As you see the crowded seats.
Will they laugh or cry or clap along?
This show just can't be beat!

The Spartanburg Little Theatre,
Has the plays you want to see.
I've performed there many times,
It's my favorite place to be.

I've met so many friends,
They are so close to me,
It's like we've lived together,
They seem like family.

In the pit there's Gary McCraw,
Always there to play.
The piano always sounds so good.
He must practice every day.

Behind the scenes is Donna Sexton,
A director of some plays.
Some will say she's very strict,
But, I like her just that way!

There's also Marty Richards,
A man who's very tall.
He sells the tickets and welcomes the guests.
I guess he does it all!

Pat Dillard is the lady,
From which music notes abound.
She's always there to teach us songs
And gives us the right sound.

In the very last performance,
A feeling comes to you,
It's sad when it's over,
And now what will I do?

It won't be long
'Til another play comes,
So practice your music
And beat those drums!

Allyson Farmer
6th Grade • Jesse Boyd Elementary

Tommy Six
Age 7 • Duncan Elementary

Mercedes Wilkins
3rd Grade • Woodland Heights Elementary

Rebeccah Fields
Age 10 • West View Elementary

Jessy Brogan
Age 6 • West View Elementary

The Place I Live

I live near Lone Oak Elementary School. In 1882, Mr. John Brown donated land, and the first school was built. It was long and white. There was just one room. It was heated by a potbellied stove. There were nails in the narrow hall to hang coats. There was a shelf with a bucket of water and a dipper from which everyone drank water.

A two-story building was built in 1926. Students walked to school even if it rained or snowed. All students brought their lunch from home. There were lots of shade trees where students could play.

In 1985, a new school was built, and that's where I go. Lone Oak Elementary School makes the place I live special.

Victoria Gonzales
3rd Grade • Lone Oak Elementary

Landrum

A warm, cozy town.
Landscapes of fields and meadows.
Mountains run behind and peer down on grazing livestock.
Towering pines and majestic oaks.
Birds chirp extraordinary music.

Zeke Rollins
5th Grade • O. P. Earle Elementary

Londonderry

I live in Londonderry. I have a lake where I fish. It is quiet most of the time, but not when the dogs start barking. My school is close to my neighborhood. Sometimes fire sirens go off. That really annoys me. I have a lot of friends. We have a lot of woods too. The Tyger River goes through the back of the neighborhood. We have quite a lot of grocery stores. We have two farms and two churches, too. There are three gas stations. My family is okay.

Caleb Linduff
2nd Grade • Anderson Mill Elementary

I Hear

I hear a lot of birds in the city
singing and chirping, as the trees are swinging.

I hear kids playing and saying,
"Let's play hide and go seek,
since there are no cars in the street."

I hear businesses selling to earn more money.
Teachers telling students
life is going to bring the best gifts.

I hear kids thanking God
for the food on their table
While teenagers are trying to convince their parents
they're capable.

I thank God that I can hear
these things in the city.

Crystal Floyd
6th Grade • Park Hills Elementary

I Am the Creek

I am the creek in Four Mile Branch.
I flow to and from the bridge looming over me.
Leaves and twigs, like little ships, float on my surface, following my path.
Bamboo poles grow on my banks, and rocks reside on my shore.
For centuries, I have flown over my path.
I run on like the ever-running stream I am.
I have seen the hairy caveman, as he leaned over to drink.
I have seen men marching through my thin body,
gunpowder floating down from leather pouches
and marring my clear surface.
The ages pass and I see many things as they come and go.
But I go on, never ceasing to follow my path.
For I am the creek in Four Mile Branch.

Forest Weir
5th Grade • Pine Street Elementary

Andrea Shattuck
6th Grade
Chapman Elementary

Blake Layton
Age 11 • Pauline-Glenn
Springs Elementary

Forest Creek

I live in the best neighborhood in the world. It is called Forest Creek. It is a fairly new neighborhood that is located in Reidville, South Carolina. The people there are nice and kind. For instance, when I'm rollerblading and my speed bearings get loose someone is there to tighten them up. Or when I block a puck in street hockey everybody says, "Good block."

Zachary Smith
2nd Grade • Reidville Elementary

A Special Place

My special place is Sleepy Hollow Fort. It is cool because it is a fort that I built with my brothers. We helped build the fort with logs that were at my grandmother's house. My grandmother helped us build it. My grandmother lives in my neighborhood so all my friends can come there to play. One of my favorite things about the fort is that I built a special room just for me. I can always bring my friends to the fort to play, but sometimes I go to my room to be alone. I like being able to decide who can come there with me.

Austin Young
3rd Grade • Roebuck Elementary

Alex Whitt
5th Grade
Anderson Elementary

Amanda Pathammavong
Age 10 • E.P. Todd Elementary

I Am Croft State Park

I am Croft State Park.
I wonder why people play in me.
I hear children playing in me.
I want to play with them.
I am Croft State Park.

I pretend the people are not there.
I feel big and wide.
I touch the trees.
I worry people will cut my trees down.
I cry, "Please don't cut my trees down!"
I am Croft State Park.

I understand why people come to me.
I say, "Please be quiet."
I dream I will be larger some day.
I try not to be too big.
I hope I will be bigger one day.
I am Croft State Park.

Kryston McDaniel
4th Grade • E. P. Todd Elementary

Courtney Jackson
5th Grade • Woodland Heights Elementary

Jessica Landers
4th Grade • Anderson Mill Elementary

Shelby Campbell-Cook
4th Grade • River Ridge Elementary

The Place Where I Live

My home is big and blue. In my home, four people live that care for me.
In my house I feel safe and loved. It's my favorite place to be.
It's beautiful inside and out.
My home never leaves. It stays where it is and has a special place in my heart.
Not being home for a while makes me feel down,
But when I do get home, welcome waits on the door.
As I pass, I say, "Home sweet home."

Tymesha McDowell
5th Grade • Westview Elementary

My House

My house is the color brown.
It tastes like a crisp bite from an apple.
It smells like a spring rose.
It sounds like crickets chirping.
It looks like a water drop from a leaf.
It makes me want to relax all day long.

Blake Johnson
3rd Grade • Pauline-Glenn Springs Elementary

Cameron Sloan
Age 9 • Jesse S. Bobo Elementary

Fire Station

I went to the Croft Fire Station.
I heard loud sirens, 911 calls, and firemen talking.
I smelled rubber and the firemen's food.
I saw a fire pole, a big clock, and the firemen's equipment.
I felt excited and amazed to see all the cool stuff.

Daniel Moxley
2nd Grade • St. Paul's Catholic School

Megan Warren
Age 7
Reidville Elementary

Spartanburg, From My Point of View

I love Spartanburg, from my point of view
It's a great place to live, from my point of view
There are lots of things to do, from my point of view
You never get bored, from my point of view
The food is great, from my point of view
The people are nice, from my point of view
This is why I love Spartanburg, from my point of view

Kathleen Crowley
5th Grade • Spartanburg Day School

Steven Ulmer
Age 6 • Pine Street Elementary

The Life of Ann Gray

Ann Gray's father owned the Gray's Department Store in Woodruff. As Ann was growing up Mr. Coleman (a local historian) thought of her as royalty. She was the town beauty.

When Ann was an older teenager she fell in love with a young man from New York. Her father did not like him. Back then New York was a very sinful and faraway place. Ann's father promised Ann a trip around the world if she did not marry the young man. Ann chose the trip. Mrs. Pansy's daughter walked up the stairs in Ann's home and saw all of Ann's beautiful clothes hanging up in the room, as Ann was packing. When she got back from her trip her suitcase was covered in stamps. There even was one from Hong Kong. All of her things went to the churches within a 20-mile range of her home.

Ann Gray was a nice lady and pleasant at that. That is why we remember her today.

Heather Hatfield
3rd Grade • Woodruff Elementary

Courtney Means
Age 10 • Roebuck Elementary

My Apartment

My apartment is three stories high
I live on the bottom
When we leave everyone says bye
We have three bedrooms
One for my mom, one for my brother
And one for I
We are all very happy here.

Cody Taplin
4th Grade • Wellford Elementary

Logan Hiers
1st Grade
Fairforest Elementary

The Place I Live

I love where I live. I live in Spartanburg County. I live on a tree farm with my family. My grandfather lives next door to me. We have a tractor and a gator. Sometimes we go on long gator rides in our field. We have three dogs and two cats. We also have chickens. We eat their eggs. We have a pond. It has a waterfall which falls in a creek. At the pond there is a shelter. It is our barbecue shed. In the warmer months we go down to the pond, wade in the creek, and walk in the field. Then we eat delicious ribs. My grandfather plants trees in the field. When they get old enough we will sell them. Next to the barbecue shed there is a pumphouse which controls the irrigation system to water the trees. We have two gardens. They produce vegetables that we eat. We also have an orchard. It gives us peaches, apples, plums, and pears. I may not live in the city close to people and stores, but I love this part of Spartanburg best.

Jordan Josey
4th Grade • The Village School

Jeremy Floyd
Age 10
Roebuck Elementary

Laura Jameson
Age 8 • E. P. Todd Elementary

Weston Olencki
3rd Grade
Spartanburg Day School

The Chinese Restaurant

The important thing about the Chinese restaurant is that they charge good prices. The name of the restaurant is Peak's. Here are some things about the restaurant. They have delicious food. Where you go to order smells like chicken. Sometimes, I like to order two boxes. When I go in, I take a deep breath and smile. Sometimes, I go in and hear Chinese voices. The Chinese people have funny voices that make me laugh a lot because their language is funny sounding to me. Sometimes, I go in and order. They will bring me my food, and I'll give them the money. They will give me my change, and I'll leave. They even have free delivery! The Chinese people are not mean people. They are nice people. And the Chinese people are very quick!

Rodrick Tucker
2nd Grade • Z. L. Madden Elementary

Sara Blackman
Age 10 • Pine Street Elementary

The Place Where I Live

I live in the world.
I live on earth.
I live in the United States.
I live in South Carolina.
I live on Thorn Drive.
I live in a house.
It is my home.

Cody Mason
1st Grade
River Ridge Elementary

Leslie Yarborough
Age 10
Roebuck Elementary

A Good Hub City Poem Should ...

Use similes, metaphors, and personifications
Have detail
Show originality and creativity
Use good vocabulary
Stay on the topic: Spartanburg County places
Be clear and understandable
Be well edited
Be interesting: no boring words!
Have a good beginning to hook the reader
Have feelings, not so much information
Use all the senses, not just sight
Be organized
Have a good ending that leaves the reader thinking and feeling.

The 5th Grade students of Mary Pell
Pine Street Elementary

Terry Vongsouthi
Age 9 • Woodland Heights Elementary

Acknowledgements

The history of the Hub City Writers Project is peppered with seminal moments when, by accident or good fortune, a new literary initiative becomes clear. One such moment happened in May 2000 when a handful of students from Chapman Elementary School came to the local Barnes & Noble store to read poetry they had written for our book, *The Lawson's Fork: Headwaters to Confluence*.

The little café was full of parents, teachers and Hub City writers that afternoon as the children came to the podium, one by one, and strained to reach the microphone. They read carefully and with great composure. When it was over, they signed books, smiling and chatting with the adults. These children had become writers, and their self-assurance was palpable.

We knew that day that Hub City's next mission was to give as many local children as possible a similar experience.

Hub City would like to gratefully acknowledge the dozens of teachers across Spartanburg County who led their children through writing exercises to produce the work for this book. Many teachers used a curriculum we assembled for teaching children to write poetry about place (available on the web at www.hubcity.org/ideabook.htm); others used their own creativity. In some cases, Hub City writers came to the schools and worked directly with the children. In the end, more than 2,000 students from 32 schools participated in this project, either by writing a story or poem or by drawing a picture of the places they live.

We regret that we were not able to publish them all. We made our selections based on a wide range of factors: some were chosen because of the quality of the writing and artwork; others were chosen to make the book geographically diverse. We also wanted to make sure that a wide range of ages was represented.

Thanks also go to the principals and school superintendents who okayed this initia tive and invited us in. Much of that groundwork was handled by Ava Hughes of the Arts Partnership of Greater Spartanburg, and we are grateful for her assistance.

The names of the many wonderful friends and institutions who helped underwrite this project are listed on the following pages. Some of these donors have been with us every year since we began in 1995. The Hub City Writers Project would not exist without them.

Proofreading was handled by Rachel Farmer, our summer intern from Catawba College, and by a budding children's book author, Jill McBurney. Artist Helen Correll provided assistance in selecting the children's artwork, and Tina Smith photographed and scanned the artwork. Superb graphic artist Mark Olencki designed the beautiful book you are holding.

Special acknowledgment goes to Chapman Elementary School librarian Bea Bruce whose enthusiasm for children's writing projects has helped us to see the impact that Hub City can have on our community's youngest citizens. It is a partnership we intend to continue in as many ways as possible.

Betsy Wakefield Teter
June 2001

Publication of this book is funded in part by the Arts Partnership of Greater Spartanburg, its donors, the County and City of Spartanburg, and the South Carolina Arts Commission which receives support from the National Endowment for the Arts.

Publication of *The Place I Live* is made possible through the generous contributions of the following:

The Arts Partnership of Greater Spartanburg
The Barnet Foundation
Jo Ann, John and Brent Bristow
Bea and Dennis Bruce
Inman Riverdale Foundation
Agnes Harris
Mr. and Mrs. Stewart Johnson
Dorothy and Julian Josey
Sara and Paul Lehner
The Phifer/Johnson Foundation
The South Carolina Arts Commission

Mack and Kathy Amick
Barrie and Don Bain
Mr. and Mrs. Stan Baker
Shirley Blaes
Mellnee G. Buchheit
Clarke and Martha Blackman
Dr. and Mrs. Robert Cochran
Mr. and Mrs. Richard Conn
Nancy and Paul Cote
Tom Moore Craig
John and Kirsten Cribb
Daniel and Becky Cromer
Nancy Rainey Crowley
Frances Davis
Susan Willis and James Dunlap
Dr. and Mrs. William C. Elston
Mr. and Mrs. Max Fain
First South Bank
Dr. and Mrs. Sidney Fulmer
Margaret and Chip Green
Mr. and Mrs. Tom Grier
Mr. and Mrs. Roger Habisreutinger
Benjamin and Tanya Hamm
Peggy Hamrick
Mr. and Mrs. Peyton Harvey
Mike and Nancy Henderson
James W. Hudgens
David and Harriet Ike
Bob and Lisa Isenhower
Monica and Victor Iskersky
Frannie Jordan
Charles and Peggy Kay
Dr. and Mrs. Bert Knight
Roy, Nancy, & Maura Lane
Dr. and Mrs. Cecil F. Lanford

Gene and Nancy Lassiter
George and Frances Loudon
Zerno E. Martin Jr.
Dan and Kit Maultsby
Jill and John McBurney
Byron and Linda McCane
Fayssoux Dunbar McLean
Mr. and Mrs. E.Lewis Miller
Nancy and Lawrence Moore
George D. Mullinax
Margaret and George Nixon
Vivian Fisher and Jim Newcome
Nancy Ogle
Weston, Diana and Mark Olencki
Sally Overcarsh
Mr. and Mrs. Edward P. Perrin
Mr. and Mrs. Mickey Pierce
John and Lynne Poole
Dr. and Mrs. Jan H. Postma Jr.
Mr. and Mrs. Norman Pulliam
Mr. and Mrs. Phil Racine
Mrs. Eileen N. Rampey
Karen Randall
Mr. and Mrs. John D. Scott
Freeman and Laurel Weston Smith
Mildred Dent Stuart
Eric Tapio and Erin Bentrim-Tapio
Nancy Taylor
Bette Wakefield
Mr. and Mrs. J.W. Wakefield
Mary A. Walter
Mr. and Mrs. David Weir
John B. White
Mary K. Wilborn
Jeffrey R. Willis

Our Schools

Anderson Mill Elementary 11, 24, 30, 31, 45, 68, 73, 97, 106
Arcadia Elementary 32, 40
Boiling Springs Elementary 20, 48, 53, 64, back cover
Cannons Elementary 15, 26, 40, 43, 80, 91
Chapman Elementary 16, 30, 44, 46, 61, 100, front cover
Cleveland Elementary 13, 58, 60, 67
Clifdale Elementary 14, 57, 60, 70
Cowpens Elementary 26, 36, 32, 43, 54, 71
Duncan Elementary 48, 58, 60, 72, 84, 90, 93
E. P. Todd Elementary 24, 82, 90, 103, 105, 116, back cover
Fairforest Elementary 25, 32, 41, 52, 62, 75, 78, 114
Hendrix Elementary 80, 81
Houston Elementary 12, 16, 27, 28, 60, 70, 75, 83, 85
Holly Springs-Motlow Elementary 21, 68
Jessy S. Bobo Elementary 2, 9, 10, 34, 73, 84, 108, back cover
Jessy Boyd Elementary 9, 88, 92
Lone Oak Elementary 90, 97

O. P. Earle Elementary 15, 37, 55, 97
Park Hills Elementary 29, 98
Pauline-Glenn Springs Elementary 14, 19, 22, 41, 100, 109
Pine Street Elementary 43, 45, 61, 77, 79, 99, 111, 117, 120
Reidville Elementary 19, 83, 101, 110
River Ridge Elementary 50, 56, 69, 86, 119, 107
Roebuck Elementary 42, 44, 46, 59, 65, 74, 76, 88, 101, 112, 115, 118
St. Paul's Catholic School 12, 62, 110
Spartanburg Day School 36, 82, 111, 116
Village School 115
Woodland Heights Elementary 23, 27, 35, 59, 85, 94, 104, 121, back cover
Woodruff Elementary 14, 18, 19, 37, 49, 64, 112
Wellford Elementary 13, 38, 39, 78, 89, 114
Westview Elementary 33, 52, 89, 95, 96, 109
Z.L. Madden Elementary 42, 54, 65, 66, 86, 117

Our Students

A
Arreola, Tesse 25
Arce, Paolo 31
Andrews, Amber 9
Arthur, Chris 28/29

B
Bagwell, Chelsea 44
Bailey, Alexis 71
Bailey, Travis 75
Ballenger, Kathy 11
Barnes, Josh 73
Batchelor, Ariel 82
Bates, Jeanette 27
Blackman, Sara 117
Blick, Meghan 74
Bowie, Emily 85
Boyd, Kiarra 29
Branch, Nathan 89
Brewington, Holden 19
Brogan, Jesse 96
Brooks, Mikki 84
Brown, Alysia 57
Brown, Brittany 60
Brown, Hunter 36
Brown, Tyler, back cover
Browning, Mary Ashleigh 23
Browning, Tristam 81
Bryant, Jonathan 14
Bullman, Nicholas 34
Burke, Katie 82
Bush, Kaitlyn 35

C
Campbell-Cook, Shelby 107
Case, Aaron 61
Champion, Landon 26
Clarke, Hayden 21
Classen, Zella 63
Classen, Zoey 46
Cochran, Brooks 61
Cohen, Tyler 85
Collins, Jacob 15
Compton, Ian 36
Crowley, Kathleen 111
Culp, Caitlyn 80

D
Davis, Christina 60
Dew, N. Chenalle 75
Dillinger, Regina 55
Dowdle, Jordan 58
Dyson, Mike 14

E
Earnhardt, Christian 12
Edge, Kayla 32
Emplit, Nathalie 24
Estes, Andrew 16/17

F
Fair, Brittany 91
Faircloth, Stephanie 41
Farmer, Allyson 92
Farr, Nikita 67
Fernanders, Kwame 65
Fields, Rebeccah 95
Floyd, Crystal 98
Floyd, Jeremy 115
Foster, Anna 10
Foster, De 90
Foster, Tiffany 78
Fowler, Ryan 70/71

G
Gaida, Jennifer 46/47

Garrett, Dwayne 44
Garza, Angie 43
Gasque, John 18
Gentry, Andre 90
Gilbert, Darryn 54
Gonzales, Victoria 97
Goodwin, Sadie 64
Gossett, Kevin 15
Gray, Andy 73
Green, Brittany 38/39
Griffin, Brandon 12
Grodzicki, Alexandra 9

H
Hannouche, Marie 62
Harris, Amanda 53
Hart, Brittany 39
Hatfield, Heather 112
Hauldrook, Alex 33
Helderman, Matthew 41
Henderson, Jordan 78
Hennett, Jake 64
Hiers, Logan 114
Hines, Kacie, back cover
Hopkins, Adam 84
Horton, Dylan 40
Hughes, A. J. 52
Hughes, Ishayda 56/57
Hy, Alex 66/67

J
Jackson, Courtney 104/105
Jackson, Justyn, back cover
Jameson, Laura 116
Jeter, Bryneisha 42
Johnson, Blake 109
Jones, Autum 26
Jones, Cameron 60
Josey, Jordan 115

K
Kumar, Pallavi 68
Kurczy, Jack 43

L
Landers, Jessica 106/107
Lawson, Zachary 48
Layton, Blake 100
Lindsey, Brittney 48
Linduff, Caleb 97

Littlejohn, Jana 14
Long, Anna Grace 32
Losey, Cassie 39
Lowery, Maggie 80
Lybrand, Kevin 45
Lyles, Jasmine 13
Lynch, Latisha 16

M
MacMillan, Ryan 52
Martin, Marylee 77
Mason, Cody 119
McCarter, Rebecca 30
McDaniel, Kryston 105
McDowell, Tymesha 109
McGee, Donna 49
McKinney, Brianna 40
McVey, James 86/87
Meadows, Jamaar 22
Means, Courtney 112/113
Messick, Daniel, front cover
Millwood, Nicholas 20
Morgan, Rebekah 42/43
Morriss, Jason 59, 76
Moxley, Daniel 110
Mullins, Terrica 13
Myers, Kwame 58

N
Nance, Cortney 62/63
Nayfa, Christina 88
Nesbitt, Markeisha 19
Norman, DeOnté 30

O
O'Shields, Amber title page
Olencki, Weston 116

P
Palmer, Whitney 19
Pathammavong, Amanda 102/103
Purinton, Bellamy 79

R
Rogers, Leah 83
Rollins, Zeke 97
Rudicill, Dylan 54

S
Salyer, Kelly 68

Shattuck, Andrea 100
Simpson, A. J. 72
Simpson, Syerra 60
Sisomseune, James, back cover
Six, Tommy 93
Sloan, Cameron 108/109
Smart, Adrian 27
Smiley, Quinton 43
Smith, Chris 86
Smith, Joshua 65
Smith, Zachary 101
Strange, Taylor 88

T
Talbert, Laney 45
Taplin, Cody 114
Theuambounmy, Petho 24
Thompson, Chelsea 89
Trinh, Melonie 32
Trojan, Travis 83
Tucker, Rodrick 117

U
Ulmer, Steven 111

V
Varner, Brittany 37
Vaughn, T. J. 55
Vongsouthi, Terri 121

W
Warren, Megan 110
Watkins, Todd 59
Weir, Forest 99
Wellingsky, Casey 50/51
Whitt, Alex 102
White, Isaac 70
Wilkins, Mercedes 94
Workman, Sara 69

Y
Yang, Cher Fue 90
Yang, Sean 90
Yang, Steven 90
Yarborough, Leslie 118/119
Young, Austin 101

Z
Zorn, Quentin 37

The Hub City Writers Project is a non-profit organization whose mission is to foster a sense of community through the literary arts. We do this by publishing books from and about our community; encouraging, mentoring, and advancing the careers of local writers; and seeking to make Spartanburg a center for the literary arts.

Our metaphor of organization purposely looks backward to the nineteenth century when Spartanburg was known as the "hub city," a place where railroads converged and departed.

At the beginning of the twenty-first century, Spartanburg has become a literary hub of South Carolina with an active and nationally celebrated core group of poets, fiction writers, and essayists. We celebrate these writers—and the ones not yet discovered—as one of our community's greatest assets. William R. Ferris, former director of the Center for the Study of Southern Cultures, says of the emerging South, "Our culture is our greatest resource. We can shape an economic base…And it won't be an investment that will disappear."

Hub City Anthology • John Lane & Betsy Teter, editors
Hub City Music Makers • Peter Cooper
Hub City Christmas • John Lane & Betsy Wakefield Teter, editors
New Southern Harmonies • Rosa Shand, Scott Gould, Deno Trakas, George Singleton
The Best of Radio Free Bubba • Meg Barnhouse, Pat Jobe, Kim Taylor, Gary Phillips
Family Trees: The Peach Culture of the Piedmont • Mike Corbin
Seeing Spartanburg: A History in Images • Philip Racine
The Seasons of Harold Hatcher • Mike Hembree
The Lawson's Fork: Headwaters to Confluence • David Taylor, Gary Henderson
Hub City Anthology 2 • Betsy Wakefield Teter, editor
Inheritance • Janette Turner Hospital, editor
In Morgan's Shadow • A Hub City Murder Mystery

Colophon

The Place I Live was a real thrill to design. I gained a new appreciation for our city through the art and words of these children. Their honesty was both refreshing and needed. Which leads me to confess that this *was not* the final design project on our trusty trio of 1992 Power Macintosh© 7100/80 computers! I guess this old design dog is too set in his ways. The beige desktop G3s will come into production soon. That I promise! I just will not say *when*. The 7100/80s still work and do a fine job as evident by this thirteenth title. The first printing of 2500 copies holds numerous other "firsts" for HCWP: first children's book, first square format book, first full color book and first book printed overseas. The display typeface is a playful font called Raskin, while the text uses a font almost everyone can remember from his childhood, Century Schoolbook. All involved with the book's production were rewarded with unlimited bottles of smooth and creamy IBC® Root Beer, a 1919 taste treat from Dallas, for their hard work and dedication.

The ol' design dog, Mark
July 2001